HOW CAN JESUS POSSIBLY KNOW HOW I FEEL?

Treasure Hunt Study Guide

By

Robin Norris Brown

"How Can Jesus Possibly Know How We Feel?

Treasure Hunt"

is intended to be a Personal/Group Bible Study workbook on the Life of Jesus through

Isaiah Chapter 53 Based on Robin Norris Brown's Book:

"How Can Jesus Possibly Know How We Feel?"

Thank You for choosing to study "How Can Jesus Possibly Know How We Feel?" Just When you thought you knew everything about Jesus…

See what Old and New Treasures you can find as you venture into this book. You will find, treasure clues and questions to reflect on, in an effort to help you draw closer into the life of Jesus.

Jesus gave His Love in order for us to see what true love really is, how can we know what it is, if we don't search for it?

The New King James Version Bible (Copyright 1990, 1955, 1953 by Thomas Nelson, Inc.) is used unless otherwise noted.

"How Can Jesus Possibly Know How I Feel?" and "How Can Jesus Possibly Know How I Feel? Treasure Hunt" Copyright © 2022 by Robin Norris Brown

All art work was done by the Author, Robin Norris Brown/Robin K. Brown and cannot be used without her permission.

TABLE OF CONTENTS

CHAPTER	PAGE
What Report? (Isaiah 53:1a)	5
What Arm Is Being Revealed? (Isaiah 53:1b)	8
Jesus as a Child (Isaiah 53:2)	10
Jesus Understands Rejection (Isaiah 53:3a)	14
Some Turned Away From Jesus (Isaiah 53:3b)	19
Was It Jesus's Fault? (Isaiah 53:4)	21
Jesus Understands Being Bruised and Wounded (Isaiah 53:5)	26
Like Sheep Going Astray (Isaiah 53:6)	29
Why Did Jesus Remain Silent? (Isaiah 53:7)	33
Was Jesus Ever in Prison? (Isaiah 53:8)	38
His Grave Was With The Wicked and The Rich (Isaiah 53: 9)	41
Did Jesus Have a Say So Concerning His Death? (Isaiah 53:10,11)	43
Jesus Knew What His Tomorrow Held (Isaiah 53:12)	47
Pages for Your Notes	50

Here, read all about Me in The Bible: you can

"And it is these same scriptures that testify about Me"

John 5:39 (NET)

WHAT REPORT?

Isaiah 53:1a

*"Who has believed our report
and to whom has the arm of the Lord been revealed?"*

(Pages 10-14)

1. How do we know Jesus was with God before the earth was made?

2. Why is Jesus referred to as "The Word" by John?

3. What report was Isaiah talking about?

4. If you saw Mary come home expecting a baby back then what would you have thought?

    Would you have believed her report about the angel's appearance to her?

5. Why was it important for the angel to come to Joseph?

6. If Joseph had agreed to stoning Mary, who else would have been killed?

7. What was Jesus' Hebrew Name and What does it mean?

8. In Matthew 16:1-3, why was Jesus mad at the Pharisees and the Sadducces?

9. What was the first attempt on Jesus' life?

10. What was the second attempt on Jesus' life?

Still later on in Jesus' life many did not believe the report about His birth. Jesus understands when you have a label placed on you because of what people may come up with about your birth. It is enough that God knows you from the time you were born and He has a reason and a purpose for your life.

"For You formed my inward parts;
You covered me in my mother's womb.

I will praise You, for I am fearfully and wonderfully made;
Marvelous are Your works," (Psalm 139:12-14)

"For I know the thoughts that I think toward you, says the Lord, thoughts of peace and not of evil, to give you a future and a hope." (Jeremiah 29:11)

***

WHAT ARM IS REVEALED?

Isaiah 53:1b

"And to whom is the arm of the Lord revealed?"

(Pages 15-24)

1. Who was the arm of the Lord?

2. Which arm was it?

3. Name some of the people to whom God revealed His arm to?

4. Who else are we supposed to tell about Jesus besides people? Can you name some at Jesus' birth?

5. The star was a Heavenly sign; there were many places the star shined down on. What was the clue the angel gave to the shepherds?

6. Why did the wisemen bring the gift of gold? Does the Bible tell us the reason?

Just like God provided what Mary and Joseph would need to care for Jesus, He will also provide for us. Matthew 6:31-34:

"Therefore do not worry, saying, 'What shall we eat?' or 'What shall we drink?' or 'What shall we wear?' For after all these things the Gentiles seek. For your heavenly Father knows that you need all these things. But seek first the kingdom of God and His righteousness, and all these things shall be added to you. Therefore do not worry about tomorrow, for tomorrow will worry about its own things. Sufficient for the day is its own trouble."

***

JESUS AS A CHILD

Isaiah 53:2a

"...For He grew up before Him as a tender plant, and as a root out of dry ground. He had no form nor comeliness; and when we shall see Him, there is no beauty that we should desire Him."

(Pages 25-33)

1. What did Jesus eat as a child?

2. How does Isaiah describe Jesus as a child?

3. What did Jesus learn from the food He was fed as a child?

4. What was the second attempt on Jesus' life?

5. Where is the prophecy that tells about Jesus coming out of Egypt?

6. How old was Jesus when Mary and Joseph realized that they lost Jesus?

7. How many days was it before Joseph and Mary found Jesus?

8. What is a possible reason that Mary and Joseph were so relieved to find Jesus?

9. How was Jesus like pre-teens today?

10. At the age of 12 what kind of example did Jesus set for young people?

11. Does Jesus know what it's like to be sick? When?

12. Did Jesus know what it felt like to be without food for 40 days?

13. Did Jesus know what it felt like to be without water for 40 days?

14. Did they have hiking boots in the days of Jesus? What would he have worn in the wilderness?

15. Why was Satan able to confidently approach Jesus to tempt Him?

16. Was there a New Testament written that Jesus could use in the wilderness?

17. What were the verses Jesus used against Satan in Matthew chapter 4?

18. Was Jesus handsome?

19. What are some reasons people were drawn to Jesus?

20. How was Jesus like the youth of today?

Joseph and Mary lost and found Jesus during the Feast of Passover. Many years later on the Feast of Passover Jesus died on a cross so that we who were lost can be found and are given a new chance at life so we can be about our Father's business.

***

JESUS UNDERSTANDS REJECTION

Isaiah 53:3a

*"He is despised and rejected of men,
A man of sorrows and acquainted with grief."*

(Pages 34-45)

1. What verses in Isaiah did Jesus read in the Synagogue?

2. Did the people believe Jesus when He said He fulfilled the Scripture?

3. Did the brothers of Jesus believe in Hm?

4. How is the society of Jesus day like our own?

5. Why did the people laugh at Jesus when He arrived to raise Jairus' daughter from the dead?

6. Why did the people in Nazareth try to throw Jesus off a cliff?

7. Why did the people try to stone Jesus in John 10:31? What Feast Day was it on and what season was it done in?

8. How was Jesus able to keep overcoming these trials?

9. Instead of giving up because of His trials, what did Jesus continue to do?

10. We see Jesus as being strong and courageous, able to work miracles and cast out demons but list some ways that Jesus was "acquainted with grief and sorrow".

11. Why did Jesus wait two days to go to raise Lazarus?

12. Why do you think Jesus wept? Did Jesus understand our grief?

13. What did Jesus ask Martha about believing? Do you agree with Martha's answer?

14. Did Jesus love Lazarus? Did Jesus have close friends and family that He loved and then they died?

15. How many days was Lazarus dead?

16. How do you think you would feel when Jesus raised Lazarus from the dead before your very eyes?

17. Jesus did an amazing miracle by raising Lazarus. What did the Pharisees try to do to Lazarus later after he was raised from the dead?

18. What was the name of the garden in which Jesus was so scared that He sweat drops as blood while praying?

19. Does Jesus understand how it feels to be terror stricken with fear?

20. What did Jesus pray for us in the garden? Did you ever realize that He loved you enough to pray for you?

21. What did Jesus experience so far? Does He know how we feel when we experience these things?

22. Are you confident now that Jesus understands your feelings and emotions of fear of being alone, laughed at or rejected?

23. Do you see how much Jesus loves and understands you when no one else does?

24. Do you understand that is the reason Jesus came…to understand your struggles?

Write out John 16:33 and know that Jesus overcame these struggles to show you that you can too. HE LOVES YOU.

***

SOME TURNED AWAY FROM JESUS

Isaiah 53:3b

*"And we hid, as it were, our faces from Him ;
He was despised, and we did not esteem (respect) Him."*

(Pages 46-52)

1. Does Jesus know how it feels for no one to understand or believe in you?

2. People don't want to see the wrongs they did, they always want to point the finger at you or someone else when you did nothing wrong. Did Jesus experience this?

3. Have you ever felt like your friends are avoiding or hiding from you? Did Jesus experience this?

4. Which disciple represents the people who have little faith?

5. Jesus had a close friend who denied knowing Jesus, not once but 3 times. What's his name?

6. It's bad to have one person end a relationship by walking away from you, but Jesus had a group of people walk away from Him. How many were in that group?

7. Who was it that when his parents chose to deny Jesus because there were questions about a miracle Jesus did, He decided to make a stand for Jesus?

8. Does Jesus understand what it is like to feel unappreciated and taken for granted?

When you are feeling unappreciated and taken for granted, go to a quiet place and let Jesus know how you feel, He understands.

***

WAS IT JESUS' FAULT?

Isaiah 53:4

"Surely he has borne our griefs, and carried our sorrows: yet we did esteem him stricken, smitten of God, and afflicted."

(Pages 53-60)

1. What was the reason Jesus came?

2. Who was Jesus before He came and what did He do before He came?

3. Did Jesus have a way out?

4. How many angels could Jesus call for to help Him?

5. For what reason did Jesus choose us instead of a way out?

6. Does Jesus know how it feels to have friends unfriend you?

7. How many men did Jesus send out two by two into the cities besides the twelve?

8. Do you think verses 48-56 are hard to understand? (I did when I first read them.)

9. Who would be the ones to understand what Jesus said? Why?

10. When Jesus talks about eating His flesh and drinking His blood was He talking about actually eating it or having Holy Communion?

11. The 70 left because they thought He meant what?

12. How would you feel if you had 70 friends and they all unfriended you at once?

13. When Jesus spoke to the twelve disciples He said He chose them but one of them was a devil: Who was he? Why did Jesus call Him that?

14. What was the test Jesus gave those who followed Him and what is the understanding of the test?

15. Where was Peter when a servant girl accused Peter of being with Jesus? What did Peter tell her?

16. Another girl saw him and said to those with her, "This fellow was with Jesus of Nazareth." Where was Peter when she accused him? What did Peter say to them?

17. A little later what did those who stood by say to Peter?

18. What was Peter's response?

19. What happened after Peter denied Jesus 3 times?

20. What did Peter remember at that time?

21. What did Peter do after he remembered?

22. Why did Peter deny Jesus 3 times?

23. Did Jesus ever forgive Peter? Does He forgive us when we mess up? Read John 21: 14-17.

24. In John 21:14-17 How many times did Jesus tell Peter to care for His sheep? How many times had Peter denied Him? Was Jesus talking about sheep or letting Peter know that He forgave him and trusted him with His Sheep (New Converts)?

25. The greatest betrayal of all was done by whom?

26. What two things did he do after he felt ashamed?

27. What does I Samuel 16:7 say?

Always remember that God looks deeper than many people will. When people call you names and belittle you, God sees your heart and He understands when no one else does.

***

JESUS UNDERSTANDS BEING WOUNDED AND BRUISED

Isaiah 53:5

"But He was wounded for our transgressions, He was bruised for our iniquities; the chastisement of our peace was upon Him and by His stripes we are healed."

(Pages 61-67)

1. What is the definition of a transgression?

2. How long were the spines/thorns placed on Jesus' head?

3. What was excavated at the High Priest, Caiaphas' house?

4. What is an iniquity?

5. How did Jesus get bruised?

6. What does chastisement mean?

7. What kind of battle did Jesus fight?

8. How is Jesus able to relate to soldiers who come home from war?

9. Why did Jesus have to suffer so much in His lifetime?

10. Isaiah talks about "By His stripes we are healed." What did Jesus say about healing? What do you think that verse means?

11. When the veil in the Temple was torn in two during the earthquake at Jesus' death it represented how we no longer receive our forgiveness from our sins by a priest or a sacrificial animal. How do we get our forgiveness now and by whom?

12. Could we have paid the price for our sin? If not, then who did?

13. Who was the final High Priest? (Hebrews 3:1, 4:14)

14. Paying the price for our sins caused Jesus to have many enemies during His lifetime; Can you name a few?

15. What was King David puzzled about in Psalm 8:4-9

16. Who is the Intercessor who goes to God on our behalf?

What Jesus did for us was: Not only did He die for our salvation, but He lived for us, to teach us what true love is. An unconditional love. A love we don't deserve. A love we never earned, nor could we. A love far beyond comprehension! The very same love He meant when He said:

"A new commandment I give to you, that you love one another; as I have loved you, that you also love one another. By this all will know that you are My disciples, if you have love for one another." (John 13:34-35)

***

Isaiah 53:6

*"All we like sheep have gone astray;
we have turned from our own way;
and the Lord has laid on Him the iniquity of us all."*

(Pages 68-73)

1. Many other animals like sheep tend to think the grass is always greener on the other side. We once had a cow who always jumped the cow gap and headed for the highway. We named her Interstate Red. One day there were cars at a stand still and a policeman trying to get her off the road. She was oblivious to the danger she was in and causing. Are people like animals in that way, thinking that if they run away from their lives they will find a better life somewhere else only to find out that they were wrong?

2. In Luke 8:11-15 Was Jesus talking about plants or people?

3. Have you ever tried to run away from your life and wished you would have listened to those who loved you and cared for you?

4. In Luke 8:12, what are the seeds by the wayside?

5. Who were the examples given in Jesus day of those who fell by the wayside?

6. In Luke 8:13, what are the seeds that fell on the rock?

7. What are the examples given of those that fall on the rock?

8. In Luke 8:14, What are the seeds that fell among the thorns?

9. Who was an example given of one who fell among the thorns?

10. Then there were those whose seeds fell on good ground in verse 15. What happened to them?

11. In reading about Peter we see that the seeds were planted in good soil. When a seed is planted in good soil does it mean it never struggles, has trials, or storms to deal with?

12. Jesus came across a lot of seeds in His life and we read throughout the New Testament that those people struggled, had trials, pain, and torment. Through those trials, like Peter, they stayed the course and endured to the end. Were they perfect through it all or did they make mistakes along the way?

13. For all those who fail at times, sin and even do terrible things in their lives, what did Jesus cry out on the cross in Luke 23:34?

14. Who did Jesus pray for in the Garden of Gethsemane?

15. Does that prayer include you?

16. How do you know for sure? Write out the first 19 words of John 17:20.

17. After Jesus makes us a new creation what are some things we still need to work at?

18. Was Jesus only tempted in the wilderness?

19. Does Jesus understand how hard it is to overcome temptation?

20. What did Jesus use to fight temptation in the wilderness? (Matthew 4:1-11)

21. What is a good verse to remember when we get discouraged with ourselves? Can you think of similar ones in the Bible?

We all make mistakes, we all sin. Romans 3:23 says:
"For all have sinned and fall short of the glory of God."
Don't be discouraged because…

"God demonstrates His love toward us, in that while we were still sinners, Christ died for us."

Praise God For His Mercy!

***

WHY DID JESUS REMAIN SILENT?

Isaiah 53:7

"He was oppressed and He was afflicted, yet He did not open His mouth; He was led to the slaughter, and as a sheep before its shearers is silent, so He opened not His mouth."

(Pages 74-81)

1. What kind of witnesses were the two that came forward to testify against Jesus?

2. Did Jesus argue with them to vindicate Himself?

3. Why did Jesus answer the first question asked by the High Priest?

4. What was Jesus' answer and response afterwards?

5. Was the High Priest happy about Jesus' response?

6. What were they doing to Jesus when they asked Jesus to prophecy about the things they were doing to Him?

7. Jesus remained silent In Luke 4:28-30 What did Jesus do to save Himself? Why did He save Himself then, but not this time?

8. Who were the three disciples who went up to the Mount of Transfiguration with Jesus?

9. Who appeared to Jesus on the mountain?

10. Did the three disciples see the two men who spoke with Jesus?

11. What did the two men come to tell Jesus?

12. Seeing these two men with Jesus tells us that there is _____ after death.

13. When the cloud came and overshadowed them, a voice came out of the cloud and said what?

14. Did the disciples tell anyone about what they saw and heard in those days or later?

15. Is the conversation between Jesus, Moses and Elijah in the book "How Can Jesus Possibly Know How We Feel?" true or fictional?

16. What did Moses really experience in his life? (Numbers 20:7-12)

17. What did Elijah truly experience in his life? (I Kings, Chapter 19)

18. Did Moses get frustrated enough with the people to accidentally disobey God?

19. Did Elijah truly give into fear after Jezebel threatened His life?

20. What do you think they talked about? Have you ever wondered?

21. What does John 1:1-3 tell us about Jesus?

22. What two things were not spoken into existence but were made by hand? (Genesis 2:7)

23. Name some marvelous miracles Jesus did?

24. What happened when Jesus spoke to the raging sea?

25. What happened when Jesus cursed the fig tree?

26. How did Jesus cast out demons? Did He command them to leave? Did they? Were they afraid of Him?

27. In Matthew 21, does Jesus show us His temper? So does that mean he got angry?

28. Did Jesus lose His temper with the Scribes and the Pharisees? What did He call them? (Matthew 23:27)

29. If Jesus opened His mouth in anger during the time of His judgment, beatings, whipping and crucifixion what could have happened?

30. Jesus could have cried out for how many angels to come to save Him?

31. Throughout history people have argued if it was the Jews or the Romans who killed Jesus. What does Jesus say about it in John 10:17-18?

After seeing all that Jesus could have done and said to save Himself, He remained silent, used self control, patience, and THAT shows us that:

HE TRULY LOVED US.

***

WAS JESUS EVER IN PRISON?

Isaiah 53:8

*"He was taken from prison and judgment. And who will declare His generation?
For He was cut off from the land of the living;
For the transgressions of My people He was stricken."*

(Pages 83-89)

1. What did the High Priest, Caiaphas, have under his house? Can it still be seen in Israel today?

2. Why did Jesus have to be held in prison?

3. What counsel did Caiaphas give to the Jews concerning Jesus?

4. How many years did Jesus' ministry last?

5. Because there was no absolute proof of Jesus' guilt, what did Caiaphas ask Jesus?

6. What was Jesus' answer to him?

7. Who did Caiaphas send Jesus to for judgment?

8. When that person could not find any guilt in Jesus, who did he send Jesus to?

9. What did this third person and his men of war do to Jesus?

10. After being sent back to Pilate, who did Pilate let make the decision about Jesus?

11. When this decision was made, what scripture was fulfilled?

12. Is Ezekiel's warning in Ezekiel 18:30-32 one we should take to heart today?

13. Ezekiel's warning mentions getting a new heart and a new spirit. Did God send someone to make that possible and who was He?

14. Was Jesus our Passover Lamb?

15. What is placed on the doorpost of our hearts that causes the death angel to pass by us?

16. When Jesus makes us a new creation, what happens to our sins?

17. What does 2 Corinthians 5:17 say?

18. What does it mean to be saved? What are we saved from?

19. What did John the Baptist tell the Pharisees and Saduccees?

20. What happens before God's wrath is released in Revelation 14:14-16?

21. What are the other two verses in Revelation 14 that mentions God's wrath?

22. When we do a genealogy search, it's called a _____ Tree.

23. When many people do genealogies, they include stories and information about family members. This is called a Family H_____.

24. The Bible is a genealogy of what Nation?

25. Isaiah 53:8 asks: "Who will declare His (Jesus') generation?

26. Like many generations before us, will you tell the historical stories of Jesus?

I end this chapter with a prayer of thanksgiving. Write your own prayer here for your family members in your future.

***

HIS GRAVE WAS WITH THE WICKED AND THE RICH

Isaiah 53:9

"And they made his grave with the wicked, and with a rich man in his death; Because he had done no violence, neither was any deceit in his mouth."

(Pages 90-94)

1. Who were the wicked who died with Jesus?

2. What Psalm describes Jesus' crucifixion?

3. Was King David allowed to experience Jesus' crucifixion before anyone else?

4. Can Jesus relate to those who have been taken forcibly and physically abused in a way that brings shame and embarrassment, uncovered against their will?

5. Where were criminals buried on Jesus' day?

6. Was Jesus buried there?

7. At the risk of angering the Romans, who risked his life to ask for Jesus' body?

8. Was there any violence or deceit found in Jesus?

9. The Pharisees etc… failed to see the prophecies about Jesus taking place. Should we be looking for more signs of Jesus' second coming?

10. Matthew 24:42-43 tells us to "watch therefore…" Why?

11. You don't want to be the one who misses Jesus' return do you?

12. Would you want others to miss that special day?

13. What things can you do to help others know so they can be ready when He comes back?

Watch therefore, for you do not know what hour your Lord is coming. But know this, that if the master of the house had known what hour the thief would come, he would have watched and not allowed his house to be broken into. Therefore you also be ready, for the Son of Man is coming at an hour you do not expect.
(Matthew 24:42-43)

***

DID JESUS HAVE A SAY SO CONCERNING HIS DEATH?

Isaiah 53:10, 11

"Yet it pleased the Lord to bruise Him; He has put Him to grief: when you make His soul an offering for sin, He shall see His seed, He shall prolong His days, and the pleasure of the Lord shall prosper in His hand. He shall see the travail of His soul, and be satisfied: By His knowledge My righteous servant, shall justify many, for He shall bear their iniquities.

(Pages 95-107)

1. Was Jesus in agreement with God's will and plan for our redemption?

2. What verse in John 3 tells us why Jesus came?

3. In your own words or if you want to, write the verse: What did Jesus say about His death?

4. Psalm 102:12-28 speaks of Jesus' coming. But it mentions nations and generations…How many times are `` generations" used? How many times are nations mentioned? What verse mentions descendants?

5. What is the key verse in Psalm 102 that is written in bold print in the book?

6. Which verse in Psalm 102 mentions "the destitute"?

7. Which verse mentions "the prisoner"?

8. God had a plan for all generations of the earth. Which verse in John 3 verifies this? God so loved who?

9. People accuse God of being cruel because He sent His Son to die for us, to save us. What examples can you give where everyday people throughout generations sent their children out for the purpose of helping or saving other people's lives? Even people they don't know or ever met before…strangers. All because they have a heart and desire to do so.

10. What kind of world would it be if no one ever stood up to evil?

11. What if no one ever risked their lives to help a person in danger? What do you think of people who do these things?

12. When did God first have the desire to restore our living souls to Himself?

13. The people of what nation were used as witnesses to the world by God?

14. How did they do this?

15. Do you think Psalm 22 definitely describes the crucifixion of Jesus?

16. Would you say King David was inspired by the Holy Spirit to write Psalm 22?

17. Which verse in Psalm 22 mentions "future generation", "next generation", and "to a people to be born"?

18. What will these people declare?

19. In Revelation 1:18 what was the second victory?

20. How long did Jesus remain on the earth after He resurrected from the grave?

21. How many people did Jesus appear to in those 40 days? (1 Corinthians 15:3-6)

22. By His (Jesus') knowledge, what would be accomplished?

23. Are the verses 10,11 in Isaiah 53, God showing His pride in His only begotten Son? In the last line of verse 11, how does God describe Jesus?

We have heard about generations, and people to be born throughout this chapter. We heard of Nations, the destitute and the prisoners. We see an example of God giving His Son to save us and how people through generations have followed Jesus' example by putting their lives in harm's way to help others. Just as Jesus was despised for His efforts to help people, these days police, soldiers and doctors are treated the same way.

What if there were no people to help others, what if Jesus never came? Evil would abound, love would have never been shown. When we close our eyes, turn away and refuse to share the message Jesus gave of, "Love One Another As I Have Loved You", we leave a lot of people in harm's way.

***

JESUS KNEW WHAT HIS TOMORROW HELD

Isaiah 53:12

"Therefore I will divide Him a portion with the great, And He shall divide the spoil with the strong, Because He poured out His soul unto death, And He was numbered with the transgressors, And He bore the sin of many, And made intercession for the transgressors."

(Pages 108-113)

1. What did Jesus go through to comprehend our emotions, fears and struggles?

2. Did Jesus make the choice to go through all these things?

3. What does John 20:17,18 say?

4. Do you remember how many angels made up 12 legions?

5. What verse shows that Jesus understood the end from the beginning?

6. In Daniel 7:13-14, What reward was given to the "One like the Son of Man?" Who is that "Son of Man"?

7. In Psalm 22:27-31, to whom does the kingdom belong to? What does He do to the nations? Who all will come and declare His righteousness and to whom is it declared?

8. What did Stephen see before he died?

9. What does Jesus proclaim in Revelation 1:8?

10. Who does Jesus say He is in Revelation 1:17-18?

11. Jesus repeats what he said in numbers 9 and 10 above in Revelation 22:12-13. Write verse 14.

12. In Matthew 28:16-20 what authority did Jesus have after His resurrection?

13. In the book of Acts, verses 1:4-8: Are the disciples still witnessing to Jerusalem, all of Judea and Samaria, even to the end of the earth? How?

14. In Act 2:1-4, what did the 2 men dressed in white apparel tell the men of Galilee about Jesus?

15. After Peter's first sermon in Acts 2:41, how many souls were added to them?

16. In Matthew 28:19-20 Jesus not only left the disciples this commandment, it includes all the generations that know Jesus as their Savior.

Now It's Your Turn To Go And Do The Same.

In Jesus/Yeshua's Name

AMEN

Write out Matthew 28:19-20 here.

NOTES

NOTES

NOTES

NOTES

NOTES

NOTES

Made in the USA
Columbia, SC
09 July 2022